To Morris and Anna Fishbein whose presence
on this occasion made it a happy one for their
friend and co-worker of many years

Basil O'Connor

# TRIBUTE TO BASIL O'CONNOR

*A limited number
of this edition was presented
to Mr. Basil O'Connor
by his friends*

NEW YORK • ANNO • MCMLII

# TRIBUTE TO
# BASIL O'CONNOR

*on his Sixtieth Birthday, January 7, 1952*

*Waldorf-Astoria*

*The Proceedings*

THOMAS J. WATSON, *Chairman*

PRESIDING

MR. WATSON
*Dr. Goldenson will now give the invocation.*

DR. GOLDENSON

Heavenly Father, what can one say that Thou dost not know altogether? Before the impulse to pray enters the heart, Thou hast already felt it. Before the words are formed upon our tongues, Thou hast already heard them. Yet we would pray—not to inform Thee Who art All in All but to give voice to the need of Thee and, in the light of Thy nearness, to see ourselves and our world more clearly.

It is good to give thanks unto Thee and to sing praises unto Thy great name. It is also good to give thanks unto men, particularly those who in thought and deed bear witness to Thee and Thy will. From every walk of life, men and women have gathered in freedom, security and gladness to express their grateful esteem to such a man and to praise his works in the world community.

We thank Thee that our honored guest had it within him from his earliest days to heed the sacred admonition to "number his days so as to attain to a heart of wisdom." We thank Thee that throughout his three-score years he has counted his days not by clock ticks but by heartthrobs, the throbs of a heart sensitive to the sighs, the wails, the laments of men and women stricken, broken and bereaved. We thank Thee that in his min-

7

istrations unto the needy and the distressed no limit was set to his kind only, his class only, his faith only and his land only. We thank Thee that his labors of love were not sporadic or occasional but constant and habitual and always sustained by a profound sense of the kinship of human pain and suffering and sorrow. We thank Thee that through his benign and far-seeing leadership countless men and women have given of their substance and their selves to the services of healing, restoration and rehabilitation.

Yet, O Heavenly Father, the meaning of this occasion will not be fully realized if at this time we do not remind ourselves that the problem of human woe will not be solved by attending to distressful effects only. Turn our attention, we pray Thee, to the causes of human travail, affliction and misery. Give us the wisdom to understand that these ills are not in the order of nature but are the results of our own errancy, wilfulness and shortsightedness. Help up to know that no permanent correction of human ills is possible without justice and righteousness, no sure prevention of them without truth and truthfulness, and no redemptive change without faith and love.

Especially do we pray as American citizens, for upon our blessed land has fallen the mantle of leadership in a time of world-wide stress and trial. We beseech Thee to help all of us, whether in a humble or in exalted station, to be faithful stewards of our bountiful possessions and to fulfill the promise of our dedication to a commonwealth established on the foundation of human rights under Thy fatherly providence, human liberty under Thy guiding law, and human happiness under Thine infinite goodness.   AMEN

MR. WATSON: *You will now remain standing*
                *while the orchestra plays the Star-Spangled Banner.*
                THE NATIONAL ANTHEM WAS PLAYED.

*Mr. O'Connor, Reverend Clergy,*
*honored guests, ladies and gentlemen:*

It is a very great honor and privilege for me MR. *WATSON* to welcome all of you who served with me on the Honorary Committee for this dinner. I want to make special mention of Mr. Clarence Michalis for his work in organizing all of the things pertaining to getting the dinner put together so that everything is going to function exactly right.

All of us gathered here feel that we are honoring ourselves very highly in paying tribute to Basil O'Connor.    Applause

Joseph Addison said friendship improves happiness and abates misery by doubling our joys and sharing our griefs. All of Basil O'Connor's friends will join with me in testifying that he has doubled our joys, and the thousands and thousands of people whom he has ever been serving in this nation and all parts of the world will testify that he has abated their misery by sharing their sorrows with them; and I think that is the greatest tribute that can be paid to any man, a man who will give up his time and unusual talents, as Mr. O'Connor has, for

11

the thing he loves above everything else, and that is service to others. I would like to go on and talk more, but I will simply say this: that Mr. O'Connor's accomplishments in this service work have built a monument to him that will live on forever.

It is now my privilege to present to you a man who will act as toastmaster. He requires no introduction to this audience or to an audience in any part of the world. Judge Patterson has had a long distinguished career of outstanding service to his country as a soldier in two world wars, as a jurist, statesman and lawyer and a friend to all of us. We are all indebted to him for the brilliant leadership he gave to our war efforts in World War II as Undersecretary and Secretary of War. All who know him are fortunate in having the benefit of his knowledge, vision and experience. I know that we are all honored by having him as the presiding officer here tonight.

JUDGE PATTERSON.     Applause

Mr. O'Connor, tonight I feel released from bondage, released from bondage because for forty years I have strained at the leash trying to tell to audiences as large and distinguished as this one, my down-to-earth opinion of Basil O'Connor—inside stuff, if you will!

Forty years ago it was that he and I were companions as beginners in the law school, the law school of that institution on the bank of the Charles. He came there from the green, rugged hills of New Hampshire, a raw youth—and I say that in no spirit of condescension because I came from hills as rugged and green, if not more so, and I was as raw, if not more so.

I am thinking of that story from Dickens where the law clerk, Mr. Guffey, remember, took out for lunch his needy and hungry companion who ate everything on the bill of fare to the worry and concern of Mr. Guffey, who was going to pay the bill, and the friend said, "Well, as the French say, il

13

faut mange." He said, "That means it is necessary to eat, and it is just as necessary for me to eat as it is for a Frenchman, if not more so." Laughter

But in those days, we, his companions, very soon became aware of the penetration of his mind, of the tenacity of his purpose, the caliber of his leadership and, above all those things, the warmth and generosity of his soul; those early promises have been completely performed by his career, his career private and his career public.

The world knows—and I cannot add to its store of knowledge—of his sterling achievements for the benefit and relief of his fellow man; the years he spent in the leadership of the National Foundation for Infantile Paralysis, a leadership that in fourteen years has meant the raising of more than two hundred million dollars for that cause brought about by Basil O'Connor; his leadership in the American Red Cross, to which he gave himself without stint or limit and from which there were no diversions.

I say the world knows those things, but I claim to have this knowledge: the knowledge of case after case of friends in earlier times, friends who had fallen into misfortune, friends for whom he would devote any amount of time and any degree of effort to aid back on their feet again for useful years and not for themselves alone. That is part of my own particular information and one of the reasons why I say I feel released from bondage at last tonight.

14

We have a distinguished array tonight of speakers, and I will not take the time myself to postpone their appearance. Mr. Watson introduced me, but I myself am only an introducer.

We have tonight one of our most eminent scientists, scholars, healers and educators, and I give you Dr. Detlev Bronk, with many distinctions: president of The Johns Hopkins University, president of the National Academy of Sciences, and other achievements as long as your arm.

DR. BRONK. Applause

Mr. O'Connor, Judge Patterson and friends DR. BRONK
who have been permitted to enjoy this happy birthday party:

If I felt it was my function to express to you, Basil O'Connor, the gratitude of countless men and women and of children, my sense of inadequacy would overpower me completely. But I need not do so, for this vast assemblage, representative of countless others, is moving evidence of that gratitude which transcends the expressive power of mere words. Nor is definition of your service to mankind required, sir, for your achievements are monumental.

I can do no more and I would do no less than simply, humbly, express my appreciative admiration as a citizen of this nation which you have helped make great. I would do so as one of many scientists who have been aided by your assistance. I would do so, also, as the father of a son who owes his lack of crippling infirmity to the institution you created.

In these darkling days, it is fitting that we pause to honor

17

a man and his institution that are dedicated to the betterment of human welfare. It is appropriate that we do so in these times, when so much of our effort must be directed to the material defense of the freedom of individuals against the aggression of those who disregard the rights of free men and women. Harsh realities require that we recognize the necessity for directing the course of much of our scientific activity to the building of our military might as insurance against the loss of freedom or the catastrophe of widespread war. But the unknown course and duration of the present international conflicts impose upon our nation the double necessity for developing our present military power without sacrificing the sources of our future welfare.

The continuation with undiminished vigor of the great humanitarian undertakings led by Basil O'Connor is evidence of the faith of the American people in a better future. The widespread support by you and others who have enrolled under the banners unfurled by Mr. O'Connor shows to a world of subjugated people, whose suffering is disregarded by their rulers, that there is still hope that human kindness will prevail.

In these times of rapidly changing social customs, it is significant that research for human welfare, concerning which I have been asked to speak, is supported by our nation as a great national resource. It is proper responsibility of the national government which previously has been charged with the development and the protection for the future of basic natural resources, such as forests, water power, soil and fisheries.

Basic research, in contrast to applied research and industrial technology, is like such resources for it provides new scientific knowledge of future value for our national welfare. But it would be unfortunate if the full responsibility for the support of science were relegated to the Government. The integration of science into American culture requires that many individuals have the status of participating stockholders in the advancement of science. That this is increasingly so is a healthy characteristic of our social customs.

More than money is derived from this widespread but untaxed participation. Participants gain some understanding of the meaning of science. They develop a better appreciation of the values of science. Thus, our citizens become better qualified to control the scientific policies of the nation.

Scientists are deeply grateful for the partnership and assistance of those outside the laboratory who have supported so magnificently the work of the National Foundation for Infantile Paralysis and other agencies which have followed its example. We are especially grateful for the sympathetic and understanding nature of the partnership we have enjoyed with your Foundation. It is a natural desire to apply past scientific discoveries for the development of raw materials, machines or weapons, for the improvement of agriculture or for the immediate prevention or cure of disease. More faith and understanding are required to support abstract research in the exploration of the unknown for the benefit of future generations.

The National Foundation for Infantile Paralysis has greatly contributed to the wholesome development of science by wisely encouraging the discovery of new knowledge as well as the application of that which is already known. Scientists are grateful, too, for your understanding of our need for freedom, which is so essential to our progress but so precariously held in these days. Given freedom, curiosity will recruit new seekers for new trails to better fields of human welfare. Curiosity is a primary motive of all scientists. You will accept this so readily that I should scarcely pause for comment. I do so because I perceive in this era a tendency to consider curiosity as a bothersome trait which has got us into a great deal of trouble between the days of the Garden of Eden and Hiroshima.

Scientific research is exploration of the unknown, and I, for one, do not understand how it is possible to direct the course of an explorer through unexplored territory. But there is a present danger that those unfamiliar with the motives and the methods of the scientist will attempt to shape the scientist's career for the quick accomplishment of useful ends. But such a practical accomplishment was not Faraday's motive, nor was it Newton's. Who among those who urge that the scientist's curiosity be suppressed in a common undertaking would say that Faraday and Newton have not justified their freedom? Most great things of lasting value, I do believe, are achieved by the daring of individuals who accepted the risk of exploring new paths which might lead nowhere.

20

There is a second motive of the scientist which your Foundation, Mr. O'Connor, has generously understood and supported. It is a motive no weaker, no less frequent but more difficult of realization than the first of which I have spoken. It is the desire to comprehend one's observations. It can be stated as a desire to bring order out of chaos.

Curiosity impels the scientist to seek new facts through observation and experiment. The urge to relate those facts and to fit them into a consistent pattern is the motive which stimulates the formulation of natural laws and generalizations and concepts which make scientific facts meaningful and useable.

I am aware that there are many who consider the scientist's desire to follow his curiosity and develop his understanding and his liking for his ivory tower as evidence of his indifference to social obligations. On the contrary, I would name social usefulness as the third of the scientist's motives, motives which can best be translated into useful action through partnership with men and women such as you who are devoted to public service.

I am conscious, too, that there is a lack of feeling of adequate achievement by the scientists of today because the consequences of the scientific discovery and its applications are not always beneficial to mankind. But science is neither good nor evil; scientific investigation is the search for knowledge to be used as man desires.

The exciting discoveries of scientists during the nineteenth century nurtured widespread hope that man would soon com-

21

plete his mastery over nature. The scientific discoveries and achievements of the intervening fifty years have greatly exceeded the visions of the hopeful dreamers of 1899, and yet, at the end of the half century, so great an historian as George Trevelyan writes of the present fall of European civilization, and optimists speak of America's struggle for survival.

Greater mastery over nature we have gained, but science also gives man greater mastery over men. Science thus implements the lust for power of those who disregard the rights of others. If human power to control natural forces would satisfy the instinct for power, science could create a peaceful world; but that promise of science is still to be fulfilled by education and example, such as that set by the members of this Foundation and its founder, whom we honor this evening. Until more share your realization of the worth of science, the hardly gained knowledge of nature will be used by both in the conflict between good and evil. As I have said, science is neither good nor evil. Science is a quest for knowledge and understanding to be applied for human use as men desire.

In these days, when we are torn between the necessities of the immediate present and the need to build for a more distant future, I like to recall the words of a great scientist spoken in a time of great danger for his nation:

"Take interest, I beseech you, in those sacred institutions which we designate under the expressive name of laboratories. Demand that they be multiplied and adorned.

"They are the temples of wealth and of the future. There it is that humanity grows, becomes stronger and better." As Louis Pasteur continued in that time of French crisis, "Laboratories house the divine torch which illuminates the world; they are the sources of the highest sentiments, which keep up from sacrificing everything to material satisfactions."

If thoughtful men and women, in and out of laboratories, were ever needed to bring order out of chaos by thought and reason, it is today. In the past, our geographical isolation from the field of violent international conflict protected us from the necessity of making quick decisions which irrevocably determined our nation's future. In the shrunken world of the accelerated present, there is urgent need for quick decisions and speedy action. But decisions and actions which are not based on antecedent thought are fraught with danger. They confuse our nation's strategy and misguide our tactics. Only by the full use of our intellectual resources, supported by men and women such as you, can the democracies withstand the dictators of greater numbers.

There was a great chemical engineer, Arthur D. Little, who once, in speaking to the memory of Benjamin Franklin, used these words I now would quote:

"This fifth estate which I would add to the fourth estate and the three others is composed of those having the simplicity to wonder, the ability to question, the power to generalize, the capacity to apply. It is, in short, the company of thinkers,

23

workers, expounders and practitioners upon which the world is absolutely dependent for the preservation and advancement of that organized knowledge which we call Science. The world needs most a new tolerance, a new understanding, an appreciation of the knowledge now at hand. For these it can look nowhere with such confidence as to the members of the Fifth Estate. Let us, therefore, recognize the obligation we are under. Ours is the duty and the privilege of bringing home to every man the wonders, the significance and the underlying harmony of the world in which we live, to the end that all undertakings may be better ordered, all lives enriched, all spirits fortified."

Such a member of the fifth estate is Basil O'Connor. Under the leadership of such as you, sir, mankind will again enjoy the bright optimism of confident mornings.     Applause

JUDGE PATTERSON: *All of us, Dr. Bronk, appreciate that informative, heartening and stimulating talk. We thank you very much.*

*Friends, this has been a big day, not only for us in honoring Basil O'Connor but it has been a big day, too, for the Western Union.*
Laughter

JUDGE PATTERSON: *That is only part of it, and, although this place is filled to capacity, we know that we are only a small fraction of his friends across the nation.*

*I would read selections, but our hero has modestly forbidden it, so I will present them to him and, in the small hours of the morning, he may thumb these over.*

*We are fortunate, indeed, to have as one of our speakers tonight a lady who needs no introduction from me—editor, publisher and leader, Miss Margaret Hickey is Public Affairs Editor of the* Ladies' Home Journal, *she is the Chairman of the Program Committee of the American Red Cross, Honorary President of the National Federation of Business and Professional Women's Clubs, and holder of many other distinctions.*

*We are fortunate, indeed, Miss Hickey, in having you here.*

Applause

25

*Judge Patterson, Mr. Watson,*
*Mr. O'Connor, friends:*

Mr. O'Connor, as he frequently does, advises his friends on what to do. He has just suggested to me that I should start this little talk by telling you quite frankly—that I love him, and sit down. Well, I do, and you do, too.  Applause

It is very difficult to talk to a great audience like this about one held in such deep esteem and genuine affection. In paying tribute this evening to Mr. O'Connor, I want to talk to you about the five years he served all of us as President of the Red Cross . . . years during which he gave so unstintingly of himself to the whole world. As President of the American Red Cross for five years, and then five years plus an additional year, as the Chairman of the Board of Governors of the League of Red Cross Societies, reaching out over the world to some sixty-five nations, he served all of us.

But, in trying to pay tribute to him, I must tell you that I find myself in a situation which not only makes me very proud, but gives me a rare, occasional power; because in those

27

years that I was privileged to work with Mr. O'Connor, I had many opportunities to talk to him and with him, but this is the first time I have ever felt reasonably certain he wouldn't talk back.   Laughter

I am quite sure that he won't be ready with one of those quick rebuttals or cleverly worded contradictions. It is no wonder that I am a bit reluctant, really, to yield to the next speaker the heady sweetness of this moment, because in Mr. O'Connor I found not only a great friend and associate but one of the most brilliant and inspiring of adversaries. He has this rare ability of bringing out the best mettle of his friends and others.   Laughter

Gallantly, warm-heartedly, when an issue is at stake, he meets it with plenty of emotion and spirit. He wades right in, with none of that detachment, you know, none of that so-called objectivity. No, indeed. He gives it everything he has, and he gets from us the best we have. On all sides these days you hear attacks on emotion and sentiment, but I, frankly, think we need more of real emotion, of real sentiment. If we are to overcome this growing cynicism about philanthrophy, if we are to get more in dollars and in effort, then we must reach the heart before we can get into the pocketbook. Mr. O'Connor has this rare gift of inflaming the sympathy of people as well as informing them. His great leadership made him one of the ablest chairmen ever to direct the Red Cross.   Applause

He became our leader in the midst of World War II. It was in July of 1944. This appointment, as we all know, is one of

28

the most important and distinguished that the President of the United States has the power to confer. Mr. O'Connor set out immediately to steep himself so in Red Cross history and traditions that his knowledge soon amazed even the most dedicated of veteran workers, and that was a good thing for them. He went to work at a time when serious flaws were beginning to show up in the vital places, not only in the Red Cross but in many institutions.

As early as September, 1944, Mr. O'Connor stated that the Red Cross did not exist because it is the will of just a few people to help the many. It exists because it is the will of all the people to help themselves.

Loving the Red Cross, believing in it as we do, we needed to find a simpler and less formal structure, so that more people could give this direct humane service. Mr. O'Connor put the honest gripers—and we had some of them—to work grappling with the situation. He appointed a committee headed by Mr. Roland Harriman, now the president of the Red Cross, and to that committee he called other great leaders of the Red Cross, like Mrs. Henry Davison here this evening with us. We got busy and, as a result, we had an almost complete reorganization, and what we have now is more Red Cross and less red tape. Applause

Yet Mr. O'Connor's work with the Red Cross transcends that organization, for it reaches out to touch one of the great problems we face as a people. I mean the need to preserve the independence and the integrity of the great voluntary institutions in community life.   Applause

What a vital loss, to use Mr. O'Connor's words, it would be for this nation to have the "whole spirit of relief and assistance removed from the sphere of voluntary action and transformed into a massive mechanical system of individual deductions and automatic contributions." He continues, in the National Foundation, to help us find the most convincing of all answers.

During his administration with the Red Cross, we raised $570,000,000. That is over half a billion dollars, actually 14 per cent more than we asked for.

His great skill in this matter of fund-raising organization, his great gift inspires us at a time when we must hold on as a people to this most precious form of all private enterprise, this individual voluntary support of our great humanitarian institutions.

Mr. O'Connor, I think this evening is also the time to thank you for the conversion of the Red Cross blood program to meet new needs at the end of World War II. It was largely because of your vision and your determination that the Red Cross blood program was in readiness so that General Marshall and now Mr. Harriman, who succeeded you, were able to make it possible for the Red Cross to serve the wounded and the ill in Korea, and to help thousands of people at home by making free blood available to save civilian lives.

That is one of the greatest contributions that Mr. O'Connor made while he was president. Inspiring and encouraging us at a time when it was so easy for people to let down, he helped the Red Cross to hold on to its great national Red Cross blood program.

When Mr. O'Connor resigned as president in October, 1949, his enormously successful administration really didn't end, because he is a great imaginative organization engineer. He knows how to lift up people's estimate of what they can do.

For weeks, for months, for years, Mr. O'Connor, after working with you, people have more confidence not only in what they can do but in what other people can do.

Mr. O'Connor gives you confidence in yourself and in others. He has helped millions of volunteers to find this new sense of purpose about their place in the Red Cross. We learned so much from his unassuming altruism, from that rare quality which the French call "politeness of the heart."

Because of his leadership, people all over the world have been helped to understand that there will be just as much peace and good will and brotherhood as we find in our hearts—no more, no less. All of us must love our neighbor, must do more, must bend every effort if we are to have that better world we want for the whole human family.   Applause

JUDGE PATTERSON: *Thank you very much, Miss Hickey. You left us here tonight not in the slightest doubt that your message came straight from the heart, and it went to our hearts.*

*Miss Hickey has spoken of the great work of Basil O'Connor with the American Red Cross. I am asking Mr. Louis Pink to speak for the trustees of the National Foundation for Infantile Paralysis.* Applause

*Mr. Patterson, Mr. O'Connor,*
*Helen Hayes and other friends:*

I bear no message tonight from the halls of the uni- MR. PINK
versity or from science but only from the human heart.

Over thirty thousand people are aided by the National
Foundation each year without distinction with regard to race,
color or social position, most of them young people trying to
accommodate themselves to this difficult world into which they
were born. Literally millions of people have given time and have
given money to this great enterprise, but how many of us have
given until it hurts? How many of us have spent our time, hours
each day, hours each night, trying to make this great enterprise
grow and prosper and be useful to the people of this country
and other countries?

Twenty-five years ago Basil O'Connor assumed willingly
the mantle of keeping alive this great enterprise, of finding the
money to keep it going, bequeathed to him by the late President,
Franklin D. Roosevelt. He has not only raised the funds to keep
this great work going, but he has kept alive the fire of public

33

interest. He had helped to make it possible for those who have been stricken to find medical care, and he has helped in this great effort of science to bring about a cure.

The door to the cure has been closed. It is beginning to open a little. Soon we shall enter.

Basil O'Connor, on behalf of the trustees of the National Foundation, I bring you deep friendship and deep affection, and I present to you this token from them.

I also bring to you at the same time the respect, the admiration and the gratitude of thousands of people—men, women and little children—for whom you have made life more possible and happier.  Applause

MR. O'CONNOR: Louis, I accept this, as I think you would expect me to, not for myself but on behalf of those millions to whom you referred who have made such a great cause as the National Foundation possible.  Applause

JUDGE PATTERSON: *Now, friends, I will simply present our first lady of the theater, Miss Helen Hayes.*  Applause

As you see, I have a very nice, tidy speech prepared here, and now I think I am going to have to disregard it. It was going to be my portrait of the man we are here to honor tonight, but as I listened to all of these monumental portraits that were painted by the speakers before me who have known him much longer and more intimately than I have, I feel it would be presumptuous of me to try to tell you or make you see my Basil O'Connor.

I am going to take advantage of this moment to pay him the thanks, to express to him the deep gratitude that is in my heart. I don't think, if we weren't in front of all of you, I would have the courage to tell him the things I am going to tell him now, and, anyway, I don't think he would sit still long enough for me to do so.

Basil O'Connor came into my life, I grew to know him well at a time of my own misfortune. I shall never forget those midnight calls to his house and on through the night when the doc-

35

tors were in need of his help and the help of the National Foundation when my daughter was fighting for her life. Through the ten days that followed, although I never spoke to him myself on the phone, although I never saw him, I felt he was there by my side through that fight. Every day that passed brought new evidence of the great organization that he heads—the doctors and specially trained nurses who worked around the clock, the special equipment, the constant care and solicitude. I remember that, when I met him two months after Mary had gone, we were in a crowded room and I was very afraid of the meeting, afraid I would become emotional, I suppose, but I looked at his eyes. He probably doesn't even remember this now, but there was a great shadow of pain that passed across them, and he said—and the words rushed out of him; I am sure he wasn't aware of them —"We did all we could, but it wasn't enough," and at that moment he seemed to take onto himself some of my pain. At that moment I found myself being sorry for *him*. But I also looked at his clenched jaw, and I knew for sure that this was a man who would never stop until he could say to every parent everywhere in the world, "We did what we could, and it *was* enough."

Applause

My life is irrevocably a part of the National Foundation, and the National Foundation is irrevocably a part of my life, and, when the day of victory over infantile paralysis dawns, as it surely will before long now, I know that that, Basil O'Connor, is the only reward that you seek.

36

I know that you haven't worked in this fight as most of us work in good causes. We take them as an avocation, we take great interest in them, and we work at them in our spare time; but I know that in this fight against polio, you have made it the fight of your life. It has been your life!

I know that you didn't just adjust your life and your spare time to it. You simply adjusted your life so that you would have spare time for other things besides the fight on polio. This was the way you went about it.

Perhaps you don't remember your very gentle and patient education of me when you were bringing me back to life. You gave me many good, sound little jewels of wisdom and advice and oh! so much humor, but I think once, in passing, you told me what might possibly be the explanation of your life. I think you said it was one of your favorite Bible lessons. It is a very short verse from the Sermon on the Mount. It is simply: "Whosoever shall compel you to go one mile, go with him twain." Yes, you are the man who will never stop until it is enough. You are the man who, when you have gone the first mile and have done everything that is required of you, have met every responsibility of the job at hand, will say, "Now, have we done all that is possible? Have I done all that I am obliged to do? Yes? Well, then, now I will really start."

You are certainly the man who will go the second mile and, like all your older friends here tonight and the people who have known you better than I, I just want to say that the world is a richer place for me since I have known you and, however un-happy it may seem to be, I am very grateful that I am living in this particular age, in this particular time, because I am living in the same world with you, Basil O'Connor, and I know that it is going to be a better world because of you and of the work you have done.

And now I want to give the floor back to Judge Patterson, who has a message for you.   Applause

JUDGE PATTERSON : *What can we say after a tribute as close and touching as that which Miss Hayes has just given us? I confess that it is quite beyond me.*

*That is a tribute, Miss Hayes, that none of us will ever forget.*

*Now I have a little act of my own to perform. For all these years I have bowed to the wisdom of the man on my left. He has given me some other orders, so I will defer that for a moment. He can make what explanations to you he can.*

*Judge Patterson, Mr. Watson*
*and my very good friends:*

I cannot imagine a more difficult spot than MR. O'CONNOR
I am in at this moment, and I know you sympathize with me
fully. It would have been sufficiently difficult without those
lovely words from Helen Hayes. One cannot do anything but
love Helen Hayes if one knows Helen Hayes.

No matter what he might have accomplished, no one who
heard the words uttered here tonight could be egotistical
enough, honestly, to believe that he personally deserved them.
Even vanity can blush. Rather than appropriate to my own self
the eulogies we have just heard—the encomiums that I know
have been spoken with sincerity and honesty—I prefer to feel,
if you will permit me so to do, that there has been a certain sym-
bolism involved in what we have attempted to accomplish that
has moved you to come here tonight and has caused to be said
those things that have been so graciously uttered.

If I felt otherwise and if I attempted to capture this glorious
moment only for my very own self, what I would think tonight

could not possibly find expression in mere words but would have to be transmitted only through the silence of our friendly hearts.

In his recently published book, *The Crisis in Human Affairs*, J. B. Bennett, a mathematical physicist, in discussing the importance of man, said, "We shall come, I think, to see that the importance of man is real, but that it lies not in what he is, but in what he can become. We all have a strong tendency to conceive our values in terms of what we are: . . . and our failure to distinguish between the values which apply to what we are and the values which apply to what we might be, is the source of much of the present confusion and state of crisis."

I like to believe that what we have been thinking and feeling here tonight is not what I am, not what man is, but what man can become, what man can become if we can but find those values which apply to what man might be. No man can have been in the field of the humanities as I have been for a quarter of a century, no man can have had the experience which I was permitted to gain through service in the League of Red Cross Societies, the American Red Cross, the Georgia Warm Springs Foundation, the National Foundation for Infantile Paralysis, Tuskegee Institute and the National Conference of Christians & Jews—no man can have had those opportunities and not have had moments when the potential of the values of what man might be were very vivid and encouraging—yes, even exciting.

May I suggest to you, then, with no sense of ingratitude, that tonight you honor not me individually but those millions of people all over this land with whom I have worked in one way or another and who are the ones who have made possible all that has been accomplished. Those millions of people of every race, color and creed, those millions of people from every possible walk of life, from cities and towns and villages and hamlets nestled behind the hills, those millions of big people and little people and people who like to think of themselves just as ordinary people—those seventy million people (think of it) from every crossroad in the country, who, through their support of the March of Dimes, have shown that they can grasp in the large the significance of scientific research and that they are willing to give support to a program of fighting disease that has set a pattern for others to follow. Those are the millions of people you really honor tonight; those are the millions of people, fine American people, whom Kahlil Gibran describes so well when he says:

"And there are those who give and know not pain in giving,
  Nor do they seek joy, nor give in mindfulness of virtue;
  They give as in yonder valley the myrtle breathes
  its Fragrance into space.
"Through the hands of such as these God speaks,
  and from Behind their eyes He smiles upon the earth."

I have known such people.

It was one of them who started me on my life's avocation—one who realized ahead of his time, no doubt, what man might be, one who sincerely wanted man to have the opportunity of realizing his full potential: Franklin D. Roosevelt.   Applause

A little while ago I said in memory of him:

"When the story is written there will stand out in clear relief, among his other accomplishments, the contribution he made to the health and welfare of all human beings through his presence and his activities here at Warm Springs, Georgia. And that gift which he made to humanity will be accepted as valid by all."

I know that to be true. I think all of us realize fully that there is a present confusion and a state of crisis in our own individual, national and international affairs. I hope we understand the necessity of discovering and eliminating the causes of that confusion and crisis. Whether we like it or not, this, in a sense, at least, is now one world, a community of people of different races, different religions and different cultures, people who are different in many respects but who are destined to be brought ever closer to one another. What we may not sufficiently understand is that it will be a peaceful world community only when the causes of widespread fear and insecurity are eliminated, when people everywhere know that they have the opportunity to be adequately clothed, fed and housed and adequately protected from the ravages of disease. It will be a peaceful world only when the integrity of the individual everywhere is recognized, when man, wherever man is and whoever man may be, is considered and treated as man with all the values of what man might be. The attainment of these goals is the most pressing responsibility that falls upon us today.

We should know by now that all the skill and all the technical knowledge and know-how of the fortunate members of our free society will avail us nothing in the pursuit of happiness, even our own happiness, unless those gifts are used to some extent, at least, to release large segments of the earth's population from the shackles of want and disease.

Many of us here in the United States seldom feel the grim impact of the struggle for existence. It is true that we work hard and with greater productivity than perhaps any other nation in the world, but our struggles are mainly to raise our standard of living ever higher, and that is good, to obtain the luxuries which we have come to feel are necessities. The bare essentials of life are generally available to all our people, in one way or another, and so it is sometimes difficult for us to understand that elsewhere the struggle is nothing less than between life and death.

In our own relative security, which we forget is the exception rather than the rule throughout the world, it is easy to become smug, to believe that all the problems of essential living have been solved. We forget that in other places fires are smoldering that can consume our own peaceful house. We are surprised to find that the struggle for existence is manifesting itself in other ways. We find ourselves involved in wars, fighting for life itself, when we thought we had those problems solved.

I have worked for many, many years with men and women who at least have had a suspicion of the causes of the present confusion and state of crisis and who, in their way, have been making their contribution for the betterment of mankind: Men and women who believe that man is so constituted that the realization of his true values requires that he express himself, not just in terms of receiving, but in terms of giving; men and women who have learned that the free outpouring of sympathy and understanding and compassion enables man to reach his highest moral activity in this life; men and women who realize that something deep within our nature compels us to give part of ourselves in the service of others.

What greater reward could one ask than just the opportunity of associating and working with such men and women, men and women who have, as Fosdick says, "The unstinted willingness to do more than anyone can ask."

No man accomplishes much alone. He must have friends to give him courage, co-workers on whose intelligence and experience he can draw, friends and associates who will temper his triumphs, share his disappointments and have compassion on his mistakes.

Such friends and such co-workers and such associates I have had.

To you and to all those who gave me the opportunity of serving mankind in some small way, to those who have shared our work, who have made possible whatever success we have had, let me say these words that have been said so beautifully before:

44

"When you work you fulfill a part of earth's furthest dream,
assigned to you when that dream was born,

And in keeping yourself with labour you are in truth loving
life,

And to love life through labour is to be intimate with life's
inmost secret.

You have been told also that life is darkness, and in your
weariness, you echo what was said by the weary.

And I say that life is indeed darkness save when there is urge,

And all urge is blind save when there is knowledge.

And all knowledge is vain save when there is work.

And all work is empty save when there is love;

And when you work with love you bind yourself to yourself,
and to one another, and to God." Applause

JUDGE PATTERSON: *I am one of those who maintain that much good
comes out of Washington.* Laughter—Applause

Before you rise in protest, hear me out, or before you try to shout me down, because, in proof of what I have just said, I have here tonight, just arrived from Washington, the award of the Medal for Merit to our friend, Basil O'Connor, from the hands of the President.   Applause

That is only the first of it.

This framed Certificate for Merit to Basil O'Connor goes with it, and please bear with me a moment more while I read the citation for which the medal is given.

The medal, as you know, is the highest award that the nation can give for civilian service.   Applause

"To Basil O'Connor for exceptionally meritorious conduct in the performance of outstanding services to the United States as chairman of the Central Committee and as President of the American National Red Cross from November 16, 1944 to October 1, 1949. Under Mr. O'Connor's enlightened leadership, the Congress enacted legislation which brought the organization closer to the heart of the American people by enlarging the base of operations and securing active participation by hosts of new volunteer workers. Due to his intensive devotion to a policy of humanitarianism of the highest order, the American National Red Cross, during his tenure, developed a program of unprecedented proportions in meeting new and additional needs in the field of human welfare, at the same time carrying out all its normal activities and supplementing most effectively the

46

morale-building programs of the Armed Services. Mr. O'Connor's comprehensive grasp of the difficult problems confronting the Army, Navy and Air Force"—the Army came first, you see —"in the maintenance of a high state of morale at all times in personnel at home and abroad, and his indefatigable endeavors to aid in the solution of these problems were of inestimable value to the successful operation of the American National Red Cross during that period.

Harry S. Truman, the White House, January 2, 1952."

Applause

I would like to tell a joke on my good friend Bob Patterson, because he has had some fun with me. He doesn't realize that the basic material for the awarding of this certificate came from him, my forty-year-old friend, and from one of one year longer, a forty-one-year-old friend, that great man, Jim Forrestal.

MR. O'CONNOR

Applause

With two supporters such as they, one could achieve many things. I have never said that I would inherit the earth, and, therefore, when I say to you that I am proud to receive this award, I mean it; but I am really much more proud that this award really comes through me to the great American Red Cross and to the millions and millions, particularly during that period of the war, that served with me and served so faithfully and so well all over this world. I saw them, I knew what they did, those millions of men and particularly those millions of women who

47

toiled day in and day out during those days of stress and strain, and who carried help and happiness and solace all over the globe, remember, in World War II; and so, on behalf of them— and I think quite rightfully—I accept this award.     Applause

MR. WATSON: *Dr. Everett R. Clinchy, president of the National Conference of Christians & Jews, will now pronounce the benediction.*

DR. CLINCHY     We have been blessed in our coming. We have fixed our vision upon a life of greatness. To the degree that we have renewed our confidence in the fact that man can serve God valiantly, as he serves his fellow men, we shall now go away blessed.   AMEN.